Six Figure Carpet Cleaning

Start and Run a Successful Carpet Cleaning Business.

John Braun

Six Figure Carpet Cleaning
-The Hitman's Guide

John Braun

"If you aim at nothing, you will hit it every time."

- Zig Ziglar

LIMITS OF LIABILITY / DISCLAIMER OF WARRANTY:

This book is NOT legal, professional, or accounting advice. You need to do your own due diligence to determine if the information in this book is right for YOUR business. No earnings claims are being made anywhere in this book or in the marketing of this book. The publisher and author of this book are not liable for any damages or losses associated with the content in this book.

You are solely responsible for your business.

Contents

About the Author — 11

Intro — 12

Chapter 1: Stand Out From Competition — **15**
  Examples of unique niches — 16

  Logo and company name — 17

  Be professional — 18

  How to price carpet cleaning — 20

  Double your profit — 25

Chapter 2: Marketing Basics — **27**
  Rules for successful marketing — 28

  Marketing budget and planning — 29

  The first year is tough — 31

Chapter 3: Start With This Marketing — **35**
  Google my business — 37

  Pay-per-click advertising — 38

Pick the best advertising	40
Why mailing to clients is important	46
Chapter 4: Low Budget Start-up Plan	**51**
Get tons of reviews	52
Hit the pavement with branded materials	54
Proven low cost media	58
Chapter 5: Stories, Scripts, Business Ideas	**63**
Tips to make clients love you	64
Pre-inspection walk though script	66
Answers to common client objections	70
Explaining worn traffic lanes	73
How to make the upsell	78
Script for selling fabric protector	80
Redo cleaning and follow-ups	85
Dealing with unreasonable clients	94
Real client stories of mine	99
Chapter 6: Conclusion	**117**

Six Figure Carpet Cleaning
Copyright © 2019 by John Braun

All rights reserved. Printed in the United States of America. No part of this book may be used or reproduced in any manner whatsoever without written permission except in the case of brief quotations embodied in critical articles or reviews.

Book and Cover design by John Braun

ISBN: 9781687537508
First Edition: September 2019

For information contact;
Hitman Advertising
Phone: **850-474-1110**
www.Hitmanadvertising.com

Thanks!

I'd like to thank my wife, Sheryl. Thanks for always supporting my dreams.

Thanks to my kids, Spencer, Talia, Mallory, and Anderson. You're the best.

Thanks to all my current and past Ad Club members. I love working with you guys.

Thanks to David Frey for helping me nail down a title to this book.

Thanks to Howard Partridge, Lee Pemberton, Doyle Bloss, Mason Tomaino, Dusty Roberts, and everyone in the carpet cleaning industry. You motivate me to do more and do it better.

Thank you Jesus for blessing me with such a great life.

THANK YOU for buying this book.

In Memory Of

I'd like to dedicate this book to Dan Traub. Dan was one of my first coaching club members, an inspiring entrepreneur, and one of the nicest guys you could know.

I received word of his passing while in the final stages of writing this book, so I thought a lot about him, his wife Sylvie, and his cleaning business. I did an interview with Dan a couple of years ago. It's on my blog if you want to hear. **www.hitmanadvertising.com/blog/interview-cleaner-tripled-business**

Being an entrepreneur can give you the freedom to do what you want and when you want. Grow your business so you can take that freedom.

About the Author

While I was in college, majoring in advertising, I started a carpet cleaning business to find out which advertising methods REALLY worked. Others soon saw my marketing and asked for my help. I was even invited to speak at national industry events to show off the marketing I was doing in my cleaning business.

I built my cleaning business to be one of the most well known cleaning firms in my area. Then I started Hitman Advertising to coach cleaners who needed help with their marketing. I've written articles for Cleanfax, CleanInformer, ICS Magazine, and an Amazon #1 best selling book. I regularly speak at industry events and coach cleaners all over the world.

I love this industry and I think you will too.

Intro

You're about to embark on starting your own carpet cleaning or restoration business. Or maybe you've started, but you want to grow your business quicker. Either way, congrats! You're making a step in the right direction.

Did you know the lack of good management is one of the biggest reasons most businesses fail? You'll learn from mistakes I've made as well as some of my clients. And even better, you'll learn about some of our successes.

Below is a bit of brutal reality. I feel it's important for you to understand what you're getting into.

Business is a risk

There are no guarantees in any business. However, you can take educated risks to put the odds in your favor. Learn about what you're doing BEFORE you pull the trigger.

There is no easy button

Reading this book **does NOT mean** you'll make six figures or make any certain amount of money in the carpet cleaning business. It's here to give you ideas from what I've done in my own cleaning business and have lead my clients to do. If you apply these principles, you may be able to take off some of the learning curve.

Chapter 1:

Stand out from your competition

Be unique!

Before you start any marketing, logo creation, or choosing of a company name, think about how you will be different from other cleaning companies. It can be tough. But you MUST come up with something that sets you apart. Otherwise, you'll be stuck in the same category as all the other carpet cleaners.

By the way, the goal is to NOT be seen by your prospects as a janitor, handyman, or general laborer. You want to be the local expert in cleaning carpeted flooring. Accomplish this and you can get paid TWICE the pay of other carpet cleaners.

Examples of unique niches:

- High-end cleaner for exclusive neighborhoods.

- Pet odor removal specialists.

- Commercial cleaning specialists.

- All-natural, enviro friendly cleaner.

- Neighborhood cleaner loved by the entire neighborhood.

- Stain removal experts who can remove ANY stain.

- Trusted cleaning company with a spotless reputation.

To make your niche more believable, you must PROVE that you are who you say you are. If you claim to be a pet odor specialist, you need to show details on how your system goes beyond other cleaners.

If you claim to be the neighborhood cleaner, you'd better have testimonials from people in that neighborhood. If you claim to be a stain removal specialist, you'd better have a strong guarantee of your stain removal capabilities.

Your logo and company name

Your logo and name should reflect what makes your company unique. It should be easy to read when it's big or small. The font should usually be basic and easy on the eyes. The colors should reflect your company theme.

Your logo does NOT have to be an artistic masterpiece that costs you $1,000 to produce. To start out, go with something basic and cheap that reflects your brand. There are several cheap logo creation websites. Look them up.

Your company name should say what you do and at least lead toward how you're different. It should reflect a benefit to your target prospect and stand out.

Be professional

If you want to get paid well, you must give the impression of a professional. There are too many unprofessional cleaners who show up with an unlettered van, in a t-shirt, with nothing professional about them.

Before I went out on my first cleaning job, I had a brochure, business card, uniform shirt, and magnet on my truck. These items all contained my logo. When I had all of this, I felt professional. Feeling professional made me demand a higher price for my service and respect from my clients. I'm not saying you need all this to start your first job. The fact of the matter is these initial items weren't that good and I quickly spent time and money making them better. I am saying that you need to have something that sets you apart as a professional cleaner and continue to strive to be professional.

Training

Yes, you should get professional training. The biggest training and certification board is the Institute of Inspection Cleaning and Restoration Certification (known as the IICRC). Before I went out to my first job, I got trained and certified by the IICRC so that I could tell my prospects I was technically trained.

The cost is normally a few hundred dollars. Check with your local cleaning supplier for classes in your area. Additionally, Woolsafe offers an excellent training and certification program for wool carpet and rugs.

How to price carpet cleaning

The most common question I get is about how to price your cleaning services. The two most common ways are per room and per square foot. Most carpet cleaners price by the room. Therefore, I lean toward recommending that you price by the square foot. Avoid using offers like X rooms for $XX in your marketing. Why? Because that's what every other carpet cleaner does and you're not going to be like them, right?

When you advertise X rooms for $XX, you're asking your prospect to compare your price to your competition. If another company's price is lower, you lose. Furthermore, in much of the X rooms for $XX marketing I see, no other selling points are made. The only unique selling point is the low price. You don't want to be among the lowest priced carpet cleaners in town. Those guys go out of business because they can't make enough profit.

```
┌ ─ ─ ─ ─ ─ ─ ─ ─ ┐
      **Any 5 Rooms**

    **$99.99**

  *Up to 200 square feet per room.
     Includes pre-treatment,
   deodorizer, and deep cleaning.
   Must present coupon at cleaning.
└ ─ ─ ─ ─ ─ ─ ─ ─ ┘
```

This is what most ads, websites, and marketing materials look like from a carpet cleaning company. The price is X rooms for $XX. The headline and slogan is overused and absolutely meaningless. The ad only contains prices and a list of services. This won't help you charge what you're worth. You need to do something different than your competition..

Square foot or per room?

They both have advantages. If you price by the room, it's easier for your client to understand your pricing. It can be easier to give quotes on the phone and in person. However, misunderstandings can happen when your client has a HUGE room.

For example, if you clean a 1200 square foot living room, you don't want to charge the same price as the client with a 200 square foot living room. So, you'll need some exclusions in the maximum room size.

Normally, rooms over 300 square feet are considered an additional cost. But when you do this, you're confusing prospects, which defeats the purpose of the easy pricing system.

Charging by the square feet seems to be more accurate, honest, and potentially more profitable. This way, your clients pay only for the areas cleaned. The drawback is your prospects may find it hard to understand how you charge. Normally, we'll estimate the square footage of carpet by finding out the square footage of their entire home.

Most people know how big their house is. Take that amount and assume 50 – 60% is carpeted if they have carpet everywhere except the kitchen and baths. This is usually the case because wall areas, bath tubs, and cabinets are included in the entire home square foot. A 2,200 square foot home normally has 1100 – 1200 square feet of carpet. A 1400 square foot home normally has 700 – 800 square feet of carpet. Your local area may differ, but figure out some guidelines to go by and use them for estimates.

Make $100 Per Hour?

Have a dollar amount for each hour you're on the job as a goal. For carpet cleaners with a truck mounted machine, $100 per hour is a good starting goal. For portable or dry cleaning equipment, $75 per hour is a good goal. Over time, price your cleaning according to how much you want to make per hour.

BIG Recommendation

Even when you're starting out, I'd STRONGLY advise you to **NOT be the cheapest**.

Call some of your competitors to see how much they charge. You want to at least charge average prices. If you're confident in your cleaning ability, charge more than average. Then, work toward charging the most in your city. You deserve it.

Your minimum charge should be enough for you to make a small profit. I'd suggest your minimum be at least $85, but it may need to be quite a bit more if your area requires a long commute or for a higher cost of living.

For most carpet cleaning companies, it costs around $60 - $75 just to come out and work for 30 minutes. That cost considers labor, chemicals, equipment, gas, advertising, insurance, phone, and bookkeeping.

Stand your ground on your price! I suggest you have a printed price list. If a client questions your prices, show them the list. Let them know these are the prices you must charge to stay in business. Never come down on your price simply because someone complains. Instead, offer to do less services for them. For example, if a prospect complains about the price being $275, offer to not do one of the rooms or do a lesser level of service. If you reduce the price of the job, it would only be because you are reducing what you are doing for them. Some clients will complain just to see if your prices are firm. Cutting your price means you'll make less profit, so don't do it.

Want to double your profit? Charge 20% more

Here are some real numbers. Let's say you're cleaning a 2000 square foot house and your profit margin is 20% after all of your expenses. These expenses include gas, vehicle cost, chemicals, phone rep, phone bills, office expenses, marketing, and everything it costs you to do business. On a $200 job, you'll make $40 in profit.

On that same job, if you charge $40 more, the job will total $240. Then you'll have $80 in profit. The job cost and expenses will be the same, but now your profits have doubled. In fact, your income will double simply because you're charging $40 more.

That $40 increase can change your business. It can change your life.

Chapter 2:

Marketing Basics

I love marketing, so this book will be filled with real-world marketing tactics on how to sell your cleaning services. These tactics are specifically for a start up cleaner or a cleaner who is striving to achieve a six figure income.

Marketing is what brings you revenue and keeps you in business. This is where most cleaners drop the ball. They get great at cleaning and thrill their clients, but many forget that they have to keep marketing to bring in more clients consistently.

Hitman's rules for successful marketing:

1. NEVER buy advertising when a solicitor calls you. 99% of the time, you'll regret it.

2. NEVER put all your marketing budget in one type of advertising. If that one media stops working, you'll be out of business.

3. NEVER stop marketing. Even when you get busy, the calls will eventually slow down. When you're slow, market harder.

4. ALWAYS test your advertising small before you spend large amounts of money.

5. ALWAYS improve your marketing results by constantly tweaking and testing.

6. ALWAYS market in ways in which your competition is NOT marketing. Stay away from marketing your price in any advertisement.

7. ALWAYS spend a portion of your budget on marketing to past clients. Your past clients are your gold mine.

Marketing budget and planning

What kind of budget do you need? For a start-up cleaning or restoration business, you will want to spend 10 - 25% of your projected gross sales on marketing.

How do you know what your gross sales will be? You can only guess. But it's important for you to know what some averages are in the cleaning industry. For many carpet, tile, restoration, and rug cleaners, you are doing well if you can do $100k in sales for your first year. This is doable if you market your company really well.

For a few companies, first year sales can be more than $100k. But for many, sales will be less than $100k. Much of this depends on your level of marketing skills and the budget you invest back into advertising and marketing.

You can't just throw money at it

Even if you have $100k to invest in advertising the first year, it doesn't mean you'll do $400k in sales.

I once talked with a nice gentleman at a cleaning convention in Vegas who had a large sum of money and wanted to start a carpet cleaning business. Once we began talking, he told me all about his advertising plan. He would invest $80k the first year in billboards and television hoping to do $800k in sales.

"That's great. What is the message and selling point you're going to make in the campaign?" I asked. He looked at me puzzled and said, "That's where you come in my good man."

He had it all backwards with no real plan. He just wanted to toss money around and hope some of it grew. **That's gambling** with advertising.

You have to decide your message and then plan your media based on what your message is about.

The first year is tough

I'll be upfront. It will be a slow process the first year. In the first year, you'll be building up your client base. In the cleaning business, your client base is the MOST IMPORTANT part of your business. Make those people happy and market back to them after you clean for them.

And while we're on the subject of reality... understand typical profit margins in the carpet cleaning industry. If you are able to do $100k in sales your first year, your net profit (the money you actually make) may be around **10 - 40%** if you are on the truck as a technician. If you are a "hands off" type of manager, you may profit **10 - 30%**. These numbers are assuming you run a really tight operation.

Restoration, tile, and area rug cleaning companies can potentially have better profit margins. I have many clients with water damage restoration companies who easily have a net profit of 40% or more.

Because of the potential for higher profits, many carpet cleaning companies decide to also venture into restoration, tile, and area rug cleaning. You can always decide to add an additional service later.

Test Small

When you're testing out a new advertising media, don't commit to a ONE YEAR contract or large amount of money you can't afford. I've seen many cleaners go out of business this way. Test it for a couple of months and don't buy into the ad rep's sales tactic of making you sign a one year contract. If it works, keep doing it. If it doesn't get you at least a 3-to-1 return ($300 for every $100 spent), **STOP DOING IT.**

Your key point and ad strategy

This is one of the biggest things to learn about doing marketing. Every marketing piece you do needs to have a short key point that your prospect gets from your marketing piece. That short point should be reflected in any of the pictures or words in your marketing.

For example, one key point may be "Your pet stain problems can be solved."

Another may be, "You'll have a 100% no spots returning guarantee."

Another could be, "We're the trusted neighborhood cleaner."

The headline may or not state your key point exactly, but the headline and entire ad should reflect what your key point is about.

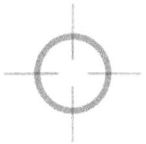

Chapter 3:

Start With This Marketing

The first thing to concentrate on is an educational website. It shouldn't be ugly, but it doesn't have to be an artistic masterpiece. The main goal is to have a site that educates clients and sets you apart as the professional company to hire over all of your competition. Use lots of your own unique pictures and videos to tell your story.

There are two reasons why you want to do this first.

1. It will take some time (usually a couple months) to get your site noticed by the search engines.

2. You want to have a place to send your prospects who are interested in your service. When they see your ad or brochure, a website will tell them more.

Website design service providers typically do NOT get your site to rank on the search engines. If you want to show up on Google, you'll need to do additional work to your site called search engine optimization (aka SEO). Allow for this in your budget or learn to do it yourself and don't assume your designer knows how to do it.

Google My Business

First, register for Google My Business

This is important, so do this right away.

Register for Google my business. Currently, you can get set up here **https://www.google.com/business**

Fill in all the information possible when you make your profile. Add pictures and videos. Then get lots of REVIEWS as soon as possible.

Here's a video I made to show you how to get tons of reviews for free. **www.hitmanadvertising.com/blog/cleaners-reviews**

Another HUGE caution!

Do NOT buy any web design or SEO services from a telemarketer or random email. I've heard way too many horror stories where cleaning companies have spent thousands on SEO services only to get a run-around.

The fact of the matter is these services can be confusing. And many scam artists get into SEO for this very purpose. Hire someone local with a proven track record or ask us for a recommendation for your web design and SEO.

Pay-per-click advertising

Pay-per-click advertising like Google Ads can bring ranking and jobs right away. You don't need to wait for any length of time. In fact, it's one of the only advertising media you can start and stop within minutes. Advertise heavily when you need work. When you are busy, pause the ads and save money.

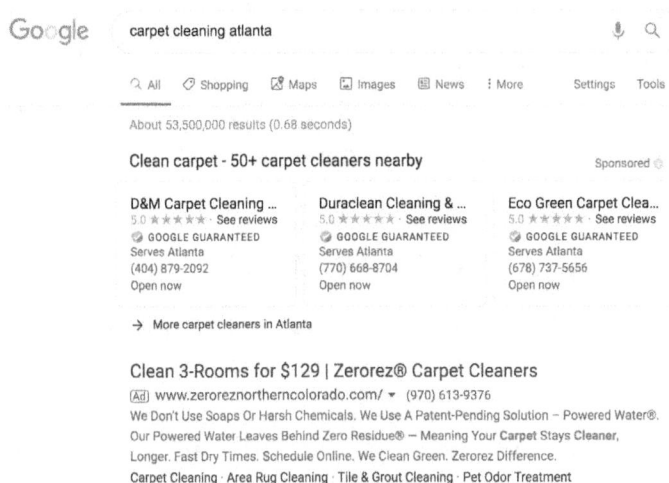

Google ads can be great for start up or established carpet cleaning companies that need to get new clients right away. There is a learning curve involved, so get some training before you spend money on this media.

I've got some great YouTube instructional videos on how to use Google ads. Look up my channel, John Braun, on Youtube.

I also offer training or one-on-one coaching to help get your pay-per-click campaigns working well. Other resources would be the "Google Adwords for Dummies" book. Google ads can quickly waste your advertising budget if your campaign isn't set up properly.

How to pick the best advertising for your business

Here's where it gets a little tricky. You'll need to do some homework to find out which are best for your city.

3 quick considerations when picking advertising media:

1. Decide what your key point (or key message) is about.

2. Decide who is your ideal target prospect.

3. Pick the best media to reach your target prospect with your key message.

This has to be well thought out. It's super important though to NOT think about choosing your ad media until you determine your key point.

The best advertising media varies from city to city. It also can vary based on your market position. For instance, if you are known as a value based company, advertising in a coupon mailer may be fine. But if you are a high-end, high priced cleaning company, coupon mailers are normally NOT a good idea.

Let me give you some general ideas on what advertising media works best for cleaners in certain situations.

Newspaper- Ideal for small to medium sized cities. Larger cities are more expensive and too impersonal.

Neighborhood mailers, like this EDDM postcard are cost effective and can be profitable for a carpet cleaning company. Postcards like this can also be sent to 5, 10, 20, or 50 homes around the home of your list of clients that you recently cleaned for.

Direct Mail- Works great to target specific neighborhoods. Also great for staying in touch with current clients. Every Door Direct Mail (EDDM) is a great way to mail postcards to targeted neighborhoods. Additionally, sending postcards to 5 or 10 homes around the home you just cleaned is a GREAT way to do targeted mailings.

Radio- Great for larger companies and/or for companies who are already known in an additional ad media like newspaper or television. Also great if you already have a presence in the area with a shop on a busy street.

Sparkling Clean Tile and Grout

Yes! Your ceramic, vinyl, porcelain, marble, or travertine can look like new. **Your dirty grout lines gone forever** Did you seal your grout? New tile rarely includes grout sealing. Without professional sealing, you'll spend hours keeping your grout clean. But we can fix this for you. Your tile and grout will be cleaned with our state-of-the-art system that rinses with high pressured water to remove dirt, soil, grime, and grease. After cleaning we will either seal your grout with a clear sealer to help keep it clean, or to keep your grout lines beautiful, we will re-color your grout in one of 40 different colors. Our exclusive re-coloring process even comes with a 10-year warranty. See videos of our system at CarpetCareTips.com Call this week and get 50% OFF grout sealing and 25% OFF grout coloring. But hurry, you must call before 10/11/12. Call now **474-1133**

Best of the Bay 2012 FINALIST PREMIUM Carpet Care

Believe it or not, newspaper advertising still works in smaller cities and some medium population cities. This ad brought in over $100k in tile cleaning jobs for my business.

Television- Great for larger companies and/or for companies who are already known in an additional ad media like newspaper or radio. Also great if you already have a presence in the area with a shop on a busy street.

Internet Marketing- Yes, great for any cleaning company. Google My Business, Google ads, and SEO are great. Email newsletters are a great way to stay in touch with prospects and clients. Facebook can be good, but not usually the best place to start unless you already love using Facebook because it requires so much time.

Magazines- Local magazines can work well if they are a known and trusted magazine. Stay away from start-up magazines as these normally have little trust from their readers.

The TWO best advertising media for most cleaning companies:

1. Internet marketing because it can get such a great response for little money invested.

2. Mailing postcards and newsletters to your past clients. Even if you only have a few dozen clients you've cleaned for, mail to them bi-monthly.

I know cleaners who have built very successful companies by doing only the two things mentioned above.

When you're starting out, you'll likely need to do more than these. But start here.

Why is mailing to current clients so important?

Never assume your client will keep your business card. Never assume they will keep the free bottle of spot remover or fridge magnet you left. Yes, these are good things to do, but they are never enough.

Magnets drop behind the refrigerator. Spot remover bottles get lost and emptied. You need to communicate with them via mail at least every other month for two or three years after you clean for them. Do this and they'll never forget you and they'll refer you.

It's sad, but your clients do NOT remember your company name.

Don't let them forget you. Nurture the relationship. Your current clients are the most cherished part of your business. They will come back year after year if you do the job of maintaining the relationship.

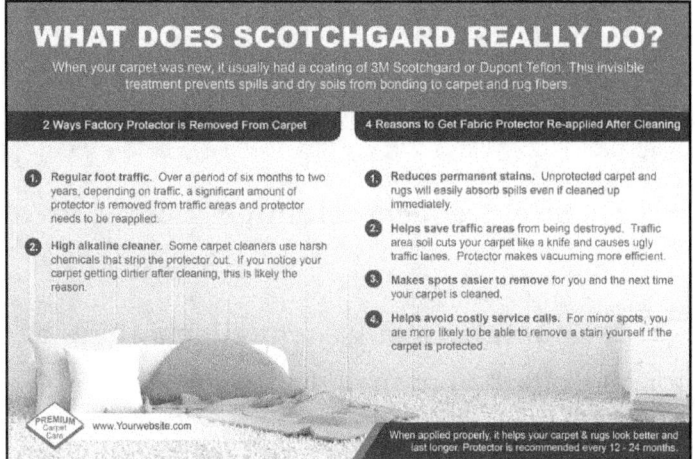

Above is an educational client mailer that is designed to educate clients about the benefits of fabric protection. Do you think your client will be more likely to have protector applied the next time you're out?

What else does mailing to your clients get you?

1. More frequent cleaning from current clients.

2. Referrals from current clients (hint, ask for referrals in your mailings).

3. Less likelihood they call your competitor "accidentally".

Tell your clients, *"We'll make sure you never forget us."*

The fact is your clients will NOT remember your company name. I can't tell you how many people have called my cleaning company because they forgot who they used last time. We tell them, "Once we clean for you, we make sure you'll never forget us."

We do this by first giving a professional service and then by marketing back to them regularly. This nurtures your relationship and is the best money you can spend on advertising.

In fact, once you get a client list of only a couple dozen people, mail to them monthly. Tell stories of how your company is doing. Educate them on how to better care for their textiles or flooring. Ask them for referrals.

The first part of your ad budget each and every month should go toward nurturing your current clients. These people are your gold mine. And after that, start spending money on other advertising media.

Start now with the practice of mailing to your clients regularly and your business will do much better. In fact, my recommendation is any time your schedule gets slow, mail to your current clients.

And soon you'll find your schedule isn't slow any longer.

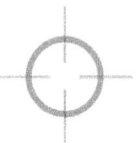

Chapter 4:

Low budget start up plan

Here's a basic plan that would be suitable for most start-up cleaning companies.

1. **Get a website up**
2. **Concentrate on getting tons of reviews**
3. **Pass out gift cards, brochures, and flyers**

Tips on getting a cheap website going:

Ideally, I recommend getting a Wordpress site up and running. Wordpress is functional because search engines love it and it's easy for anyone to use. With little training, you could figure it out.

Go to my resources page for a list of hosting companies I recommend where you can easily set up a Wordpress site. **https://www.hitmanadvertising.com/resources**

Avoid the do-it-yourself packages on sites like Godaddy if you can. But if you can't afford any other site, give it a try. No, it's NOT what I recommend as a long-term website. But it's cheap and better than nothing. Instead, either go with someone local who you personally know is proven to deliver quality websites or contact my office to point you in the right direction.

Get tons of reviews

Work on Google My Business first.

Google My Business is the most important one. **https://www.google.com/business**

Then, concentrate on Facebook reviews. After that, look at the other popular review sites in your area and get more reviews there.

Use Facebook Marketplace to post your special offers for FREE. If you have at least a few reviews and videos on your page, it can work better. But beware that the buyers here are normally after cheap priced cleaning, so only use this method if you need FREE marketing.

Also, post to your Google My Business page every week. Post pics, videos, and respond to all the reviews. Here's a video on how you get reviews FREE **https://www.hitmanadvertising.com/blog/cleaners-reviews**

Pass out gift cards, brochures, and flyers

Get some cheap gift cards printed up that you can pass out to realtors, carpet retailers, property managers, insurance agents, or anyone who can refer your business. The gift cards are to be used toward their first service. Allow them to be passed out to anyone. This way, they are giving a gift to their clients and you're providing the gift. See this video at **www.hitmanadvertising.com/blog/referrals-from-realtors**

An educational brochure can set your company apart as a true professional. Create some brochures on various services like pet stain removal, upholstery, or any service. See **www.Cleaningbrochures.com** for some of my examples.

Hit the pavement with your branded materials

1. Visit at least 20 Realtors, Flooring Retailers, Interior Designers and other businesses that are in a position to refer you each week. You'll want to bring them your beautifully printed gift cards, brochures and flyers. But the main purpose of visiting them is to bring them EDIBLE TREATS! Everyone likes food. Stop by and bring pre-packaged cookies, candy or other treats. Spend no more than $2-$4 per business. Put the treats in a small gift bag that you can purchase at Uline.com or Wal-mart.

Brochures help to educate and set you apart from your competition. The low priced, bait and switch cleaner doesn't bother with the expense or care about printing up brochures to give his clients.

When you walk in, say, "Hi, I'm (Your Name) with (Your Company Name). I just wanted to stop by and give you these goodies." Then hand them the goodie bag and smile. At that instant, all the tension is gone and they are glad you stopped by. Then hand them your brochure and give them a 30-second commercial (no longer) about your business. If it seems they want to talk more, answer their questions. If they don't want to talk more, thank them for their time and leave.

Stop by to see this same client every month. The goal here is to develop a relationship.

2. Visit 20 commercial prospects each week using the same principle in #1 using treats. Pick the higher end properties that you REALLY want. For best results, send an attention-getting sales letter BEFORE you go call or visit.

3. Pass out 500 flyers each week in high-end neighborhoods. I'm NOT talking about doorknob hangers. Instead pass out a package of your gift card, brochure and flyer that is placed in a plastic bag that goes on the doorknob. Make sure the flyer has a killer headline and compelling offer. This package will get MUCH better response than just a doorknob hanger. Check your local laws on where this is appropriate. As well, be aware that you do NOT want to place these packages in mailboxes as it is illegal to put anything inside a mailbox.

When you visit a real estate office or commercial account, bring a gift bag with a couple edible treats. Everyone loves gifts, so come as the bearer of gifts instead of a salesman.

4. Create a YouTube video every week. It can be a demo video of your cleaning process, testimonial video, intro video from the owner, or anything that helps sell. Have the keywords and title of the video relate to your service and city (i.e. "Carpet Cleaning Atlanta", "Pet Stain Removal Atlanta", etc.).

5. Connect with people on Facebook and LinkedIn. Join their conversation and then post special offers. Be careful though, as this may not be the way you want to continually build your business. It's time consuming and it isn't for everyone.

This is a good place to start. As soon as you can spend a little money, use other media like these.

Then do these other proven media ASAP:

1. Send Postcards to Your Current Clients. Do NOT ignore this! Even if you only have a few clients on your database, send something to them. Do this and you'll get more referrals, more frequent cleaning from clients and higher job tickets because your clients are better educated. Send a postcard at LEAST every other month to all the clients you've done business with in the past two years. This is the MOST important thing you can do to grow your brand!

Use gift cards as a promotional tool. Give them out to clients, realtors, property managers, flooring retailers, and businesses who can give them to their clients.

2. Email newsletters to past clients. This is cheap to do. Use a service like Constant Contact or Aweber.

Email Marketing

Sign up.
Get an email service provider that suits your needs

Collect emails.
Get client emails and set a sign up form to opt-in on your site

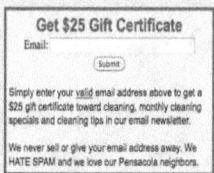

Set autoresponder
When a new user signs up, they get a series of emails on set days

Send broadcasts
Emails sent to your entire list at one time are broadcasts. Send once every week or two

3. **Neighborhood marketing.** If it's in your budget, this is the BEST way to target high-end neighborhoods. You can send large postcards to any mail route for as little as 16 cents per home through a program called EDDM. Send 200-2500 EDDM pieces each month to neighborhoods you

really want to reach. You can also mail 10 or 20 of the homes around the home of your ideal clients. We've got programs in place that can help you do this. Just ask.

4. Run Google ads. Maybe consider Facebook ads, but Google ads are more predictable.

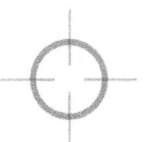

Chapter 5:

Stories, scripts, and business ideas

First, I'll go over a few policies that I implemented in my cleaning business that I've found to help my company charge more and gain loyal clients.

Feel free to adopt these policies in your own business. If you have employees, I'd highly recommend you write policies out and give them to new and existing employees. This will help your business run more smoothly and be more professional.

Tips to make your client LOVE you and your company

1. **Smile every time you look at them.** Be happy to be in their home.

2. **Agree with them even if they're wrong.** Never argue for any reason.

3. **Show up on time** (call ahead if late) looking neat and ready to work.

4. **Wear booties when you enter** their home or use a walk off mat.

5. **Bring in clean tools.** Clean the wands, vacuums, and all tools well.

6. **Ask before you do anything.** "Can I turn that ceiling fan on?"

7. **Show caution and care for everything in their home.** If you're worried about harming something, let the client know and ask if you

may move it for them or have them move it.

8. **Use poker chips or stickers to mark the spots** they are concerned about.

9. **Don't look as if you're in a hurry.** Show the client that you are spending all the time necessary to do a proper job.

10. **Whistle while you work.** It's corny, but it helps you stay in good spirits and shows your client that you are happy to be working for them.

11. **Let them see you on your hands and knees working** on a problem spot or checking the carpet for dryness. Get down in an entryway with a towel and spot cleaner and do some work in front of them.

If you do all of these things, how could a client not love you?

Pre-Inspection walk through before the cleaning

This is a basic script we used before the cleaning. It's designed to gather information and get to know your client's needs.

1. Get to know the client by asking these questions:

• "Can you show me the areas we are cleaning?"

• How old is this carpet? (Give them an educational brochure **www.cleaningbrochures.com**)

• Do you happen to know the fiber type or floor type?

• When was the last time the carpet has been cleaned?

• Feel the floor. If you can determine the

type of floor, inform the client.

• Will we be moving furniture or cleaning around furniture?

• Give them at least one compliment while getting to know them.

2. Find out what you can do for them:

• Ask client to point out spots they're concerned about.

• Have any of these spots returned after past cleaning?

• Explain your guarantee and your reputation. This may be a good time to plant a seed asking for an online review.

• Explain the steps of your cleaning process as it relates to their situation.

• Here's my formula for explaining what CAN or CANNOT be done. Explain what you can do for them (how you'll take care of their problems) and then explain what you can't do (which spots may not come out). I found it's best to first tell them what you're going to try to do to solve their problem and then let them know what you may NOT be able to do.

3. Get agreement to perform the cleaning:

• Let client know you'll be measuring all carpeted areas.

• Get client to sign your work order after you've given the price and explained what spots may be permanent.

When you're done with the inspection, ask...

• Is there any furniture prone to break when we move it?

• We also do tile and rugs. Did you want anything else done while we're here?

- Are there any more questions before we begin with the cleaning?

After your information gathering is complete, ask her to show you the areas she is concerned about (if she hasn't done so already).

IMPORTANT: Write any exclusions or exceptions on the work order that your client signs. If there's bad urine, blood, or any kind of soil that may require more work, write it down on the work order that more work or replacement may be needed.

If you don't write it on the work order that the client signs, the client will usually not remember that you said it.

WRITE IT DOWN.

Answers to common client objections

Here are some scripts that may help.

When they compare your price to another company: "All carpet cleaning companies aren't the same!" "We have an incredible reputation in the area, and guarantees that no other company has" and "We do more for you in our service than your average carpet cleaning company."

"The company that charges cheap prices likely does cheap work and has cheap, ineffective equipment. We bring the best professional equipment to your home and give you a 100% guarantee. We can't afford to do a quality job and charge anything less."

You could also reply with, "Is it important that the company you work with is certified and trained to clean carpets?" or "Is it important to you that the company you choose does a thorough cleaning process?"

You're expensive or that's expensive: "Yes, would you like to know why? Our reputation is the best in town. Our experience is extensive. Our education is much more entailed. Our systems and equipment far outweigh our competitors."

Our guarantees are stronger than any other company. Our chemicals are top of the line. The cheaper cleaners can't do all this for you because they're forced to cut corners.

Do you guarantee that all the stains will come out? "With the experience and training our company has, we are known for being able to get out difficult spots. If a spot is removable, we have what it takes to get it out. Our vans are stocked with every specialty spotting agent known to our industry.

However, please understand there are some things that can cause a permanent stain. They include, but are not limited to, things with color, like red, yellow, blue or green. 90% of brown or black spots are oil based and are easily removed. Spots with red, yellow, blue, or other colors have a much smaller chance of removal. If a stain doesn't come out with cleaning, we do have options to spot dye for a small extra charge."

Questions about your guarantee: "Yes, we have a 100% Guarantee: If you're not happy it's free. We give you a pre-inspection to let you know beforehand what we can or cannot do. This way, you know what to expect out of the cleaning.

We are experienced with several different pre-spotters to get out problem stains and you're going to see that we do more than most cleaners. But occasionally, some stains can be permanent. Some certain stains may be excluded from our guarantee. We'll let you know if there are any exclusions in the pre-inspection."

Explaining worn traffic lanes

Sometimes a client may expect traffic lanes to look new after cleaning. First, explain everything you'll do with the cleaning. Explain you'll work extra hard on these traffic lanes (what you can do). Point to the area, get on your knees and feel the carpet. Tell them exactly what you're going to do to help with the traffic areas and then let them know what you can't do.

A worn traffic lane is one of the hardest things to explain to some clients.

If the carpet is light colored, say, "We tell all of our clients any time a light-colored fiber appears darker in a particular area, it can be lightened up with cleaning, but there may be damage done and the fiber may never look like the original color again."

The solution: Clean regularly to prevent damage to light colored fibers and have fabric protector applied. In this way, you're gently letting them know they waited too long. NEVER tell them directly that it's their fault.

If they still don't understand, explain how a white t-shirt gets really dirty fast. If the t-shirt isn't washed immediately, it can permanently stain no matter how much bleach you use and how many times you wash it.

Traffic wear is SCRATCHED, DAMAGED fiber. Cleaning will remove the dirt, but won't take scratches out of their fiber.

The test to see if it's dirt or traffic lane wear…

The traffic lane test

Only do this for a client who doesn't understand that the traffic lanes have wear.

To prove they have wear or damage and not dirt, get a wet, white towel and rub the towel on the traffic area. Ask the client "Wouldn't you agree that dirt would be on this towel?" Show them that there is no dirt on the towel.

If you can see dirt on the towel, the traffic lane could use more cleaning. Clean it again. If there's no dirt, it should prove the traffic lane is clean and what you are seeing is damage to the carpet fibers.

Return a question with a question

This is a great communication and sales tool. Instead of aimlessly speaking about what you may not fully understand, ask more questions.

In fact, when you do this, you're accomplishing a few things:

1. You gain clarity. You're collecting data to better help your client.

2. You buy yourself time to think of an intelligent answer. While the client is talking, you have a minute to listen and think of a good answer to her question.

3. Your client sees that you care. By asking more questions, you show your client that you care about her situation.

A client may walk up while you're in the middle of cleaning and ask, "Aren't you going to move that entertainment center?"

Of course, you'll be at a loss for words. But don't just say yes or make excuses. Ask, "Did you want us to move that entertainment center?" Now you have time to think and you'll get their feedback. By the way, it's a good idea to have a policy for things like moving huge items.

Tips to upsell—The most profitable sale

You've already done the work of driving out to the house, meeting the client, and setting up your equipment.

How much more time will it take to apply protector or clean a sofa? Add-on sales are your biggest money-maker.

How to make the upsell….

- **Position yourself as a consultant**
- **Use a scripted selling system**

- **Use educational brochures or flyers—let it do the selling for you.**

Get over the FEAR. No one, unless they are completely rude, will be upset with you for offering add-on services if you do it right. And if they are rude, just explain to them that you were simply letting them know what else we have to offer. It's their problem, not yours.

The ONLY WAY to make an upsell is to ASK for the sale! It NEVER hurts to ask. Make sure you always offer fabric protector, grout sealer, and let them know what other services you do.

While your client is signing the work order approval, go ahead and let her know that "We also do upholstery, leather, area rugs, and tile and grout cleaning. So, please keep that in mind."

Then, stop and see what the client has to say. It just plants a seed for more cleaning either that day or someday soon.

Fear of Loss is the most powerful motivator. Tell the Client the benefits of getting the room cleaned that they are thinking about NOT cleaning. Let them know that carpet makers recommend cleaning every 1-2 years and that a carpet will last much longer and look much better if it is cleaned before it appears dirty.

Use illustrations or stories. I love to compare carpet protection or cleaning to an automobile. People understand cars, but carpet is a mystery. Explain that protection is comparable to waxing your car.

Explain that their white carpet needs to be cleaned very often so that it never appears overall dirty just as a white t-shirt will permanently stain if it ever gets too dirty.

Script for selling fabric protector

You can easily make $50 - 100 in just 15 minutes by applying fabric protector. If you don't offer it, you are walking away with money on the table.

Talk about protector after you have been a consultant and gathered all the information you can about your client's carpet and particular situation. You will present fabric protector as a solution to their problem.

On some occasions, you will want to talk about protector right after she has let you know about her soil problems in a particular room, and on other occasions you will mention protector when you are giving the total square footage and exact cleaning price.

You will want to relate how protector will benefit them to the problem they are having with their carpet. **ALWAYS ASK IF THEY WANT IT**

Fabric protection is one of the most profitable sales a carpet cleaner can make.

EVEN IF YOU DON'T THINK THEY'LL BUY. If you don't ask, they'll never know you can apply it for them.

Sell by asking "Are you aware of the benefits of fabric protection?"

"When your carpet was new it had a Scotchgard or Dupont Teflon protector in it. As the years go by the protector wears out, which is some of the reason that you have probably noticed your carpet not holding up as well. The Scotchgard and Dupont companies recommend reapplying a protector every two years to put back some of the stain-resistancy it once had.

Especially if your carpet is more than two years old, it will help protect it from some of the (name soda spills, urine spots or whatever type of spot they are having trouble with)."

Sell by recommendation:

"Mrs. Jones, I would recommend to at least have your high traffic areas done in your living room and hall, but it would be a good idea to protect the other rooms that you use as well." Then go into the reasons they should get protector.

Furniture moving tips

Damaging furniture is one of our biggest liabilities. If we encourage clients to NOT move furniture, our liability is reduced. But when we have to move furniture, taking extreme caution is very important.

Before the cleaning starts, ask your client which pieces of furniture they want moved. NEVER move something they didn't ask to have moved. This can prevent your client from getting upset and prevent breaking furniture that is weak.

How to move furniture to assure no one or nothing gets harmed:

1. Don't bend your back, bend your legs.

2. Move the furniture as close to where it belongs as possible.

3. Never move a table with something on it. Remove items first.

4. Don't move risky pieces of furniture that may break.

5. Place tabs under ALL questionable furniture. Furniture stains are PERMANENT.

We give discounts or charge less if we don't have to move furniture. In many homes, we have nothing to move. If furniture moving is selected, we can move sofas, chairs, and tables. We only move dressers, china cabinets, and buffets if they are empty (unless they are very small). We don't move beds unless a small extra charge is added. We can clean under most beds with our turbine vacuum if we talk the client into us vacuuming under the bed instead of moving it.

BE CAREFUL when moving furniture on hard floors. Some floors will scratch very easily when furniture is slid over it.

Redo cleaning and follow-up cleaning

For the ultimate customer service, you really should return to a client's job any time they are unhappy.

Free follow up appointments do three things for your company:

1. Provides a marketing advantage because many companies will not return if there is a problem.

2. Sets our clients at ease when they are thinking of hiring us.

3. Can eliminate a lot of bad online reviews, bad worth of mouth, and instead gain a happy client for life.

It is the job of the lead technician to make sure the client is happy with the job BEFORE the cleaning crew leaves. This is done by doing a thorough pre-inspection to inform them of what may or may not be accomplished with the cleaning.

Just as importantly, the post inspection is done to show the client what did and didn't come out with the cleaning. If spots are still present, the client should know about it before you leave the home. Call the client on the phone if needed.

One to three days after the cleaning, the client receives a call from our office to ask if they are happy with the job. If they are unhappy for any reason and if they would like us to return, we will return FREE of charge for a follow-up.

The only occasions we do NOT return is when the job is filthy and we inform them BEFORE the cleaning that there are no guarantees on the job.

Three reasons why the client may want us to return:

1. A spot has legitimately returned that they are unhappy with. This can sometimes be alleviated by a more thorough cleaning.

2. A stain is still present that was not able to be removed. This could have been alleviated by showing the client you did everything possible to remove the stain, but nothing can be done.

3. The client is being unreasonable. This cannot be alleviated and will happen on rare occasion.

Regardless, we return for a follow-up cleaning at no charge. This is one of the best things you can do to build a great reputation.

Dealing with flooded carpet and floors

Many carpet cleaners start doing water damage restoration because clients call when their carpet is wet. It's fine to go in and extract as much water as possible for your client. Make sure you charge them more than carpet cleaning because it's much more time consuming.

After the extraction, drying equipment needs to be brought in and monitored. You should refer the drying to a qualified water damage company until you learn how to properly take care of drying jobs as their is much liability if the job is not done thoroughly.

Dealing with area rugs

First, get trained on the technical aspects of rug cleaning, then start cleaning them. Rugs can be easily damaged if they're cleaned improperly.

Floods can be very lucrative for a carpet cleaning business. Extracting water from carpet, floors, and rugs is easy money. But make sure you get fully trained before you do any drying of a structure.

Area rug cleaning should be marketed slightly different than carpet cleaning. You can upsell area rug cleaning once in the home. Additionally, postcards can be sent to educate clients. Google ads are also great for getting rug cleaning clients.

Networking groups

Networking groups like BNI, Chamber of Commerce, and others can bring you leads. But they are very time consuming. They typically cost a few hundred dollars to join, but the real cost is your time. In the beginning, this could be useful for you to meet other business owners. But as soon as you realize it's not getting the return needed for your time spent, cut it out.

Give an estimate on the phone or in person?

You could do both. It depends on how big the job is and how convenient it is to give an estimate. If we're swamped with work, we'll give an estimate on the phone for almost any job. If it's a job under $200, we'll likely give an estimate on the phone. If it's a $250+ job for a first-time client, we would give an on location estimate if the client wants one.

You'll likely close more jobs with an in-home estimate, so do them if you have time.

Don't cut marketing when you're slow

Do what your competition is NOT doing. They cut marketing in the slow time. You should increase or stay the same with your marketing unless you're in an area where there's constantly snow on the ground throughout the winter. In every other case, give your best offers during slow times and stay busy.

Stories on how to communicate with clients

I've already mentioned that it's important to communicate BEFORE the cleaning about any possible negative outcome. It's also important to communicate and find out what your client REALLY wants.

One client initially asked me about vacuuming beneath her bed. I told her we could do that if she removed all the boxes and stuff from underneath the bed.

While I was cleaning in the bedroom, she came in and told me she didn't have time to move the stuff out. I said, "Okay," assuming she meant that we wouldn't be cleaning under the bed.

But she assumed my okay meant that we would take the time to move all her dozen boxes out from underneath the bed and vacuum.

Later, in the post inspection, she was surprised we didn't move the boxes. Likewise, I was surprised that she thought they would get moved.

Who was at fault? Well, I took the blame and moved the boxes. Sometimes the best policy is to take the blame and just get the work done.

Develop written policies and procedures for every situation imaginable

If your client wants a king-sized bed moved from downstairs to upstairs, will you do it?

If she wants eight piles of dog feces picked up in the living room, is there an extra charge?

If your client isn't home when you arrive, what will you do?

If you arrive in the home and the only person

there is the 13-year-old daughter, do you enter the home and start cleaning?

Written policies and procedures help you and your employees deal with most situations that arise.

Dealing with rude or unreasonable clients

Most of our clients are great, but when that one rude client comes up, you need to know how to deal with them.

Red Flags of a Problem Client

1. Complaining excessively about the price.

2. Not trusting, believing, or listening to your professional opinion.

3. Getting upset with you about the way you normally do business.

Every single client who was a problem displayed one or more of these red flags. Learn these flags and you'll see what I mean. You can avoid a problem client early on.

If a client goes overboard in the angry or rude department, realize you don't have to put up with it. But if you DO put up with them, it normally means more abuse in the way of callbacks, bad reviews, or refunds. With rude or unreasonable clients, it's best to walk away.

They may truthfully be upset over something we've done or they're just having a bad day. But also, know that some people will use one little thing you did wrong in order to abuse you for the rest of the time you are in their home.

Give them the benefit of the doubt the first two times. If problems persist, reevaluate the situation. You may be better off not cleaning for them than going through with the job and giving them their money back later.

Client who wouldn't stop complaining about the price

On one occasion, a client excessively complained about the price. She didn't want to listen to me about the condition of her traffic lanes either. I knew she'd complain later.

While we were setting up, I walked over to her and said, "I'm sorry. Did we do something wrong? We feel uncomfortable about being here and it seems you don't want us here. Should we go ahead and leave?"

She apologized and said she was just having a bad day. All was well from that point on. Don't put up with rudeness.

How to get the best clients? Train them to be good clients

We all want the best clients who are easy to deal with, right? All of the top companies train their clients. When you go into Starbucks, you quickly get the idea that you need to learn their exclusive menu, order, and get down the line or their employees and other clients will look at you like you're an alien.

Tell your client, "You're being weird!"

This is what we tell our clients when they ask for something abnormal. Of course, we tell them this in a tactful way, but in a nutshell, we tell them they're being different from our other clients. Then we let them know the normal way we do business.

For most people, this is a quick reality check and it points them back in the right direction. Often they're not trying to give you a hard time. In fact, our response is more of an education.

For example, if a client calls and wants cleaning booked tomorrow, we let them know that most of our jobs are booked a week or two in advance.

Whether we have an opening or not, we inform them of our tight schedule. Why? We don't want them to call at the last minute again next time.

Clients complain about strange things

On one occasion, a client complained that I was vacuuming her carpet with a vacuum that was used in someone else's home. My vacuum was fairly new and looked squeaky clean. But she still complained.

Our response when we hear an off-the wall complaint: "Oh, none of our other clients have ever asked about that." Or we'll say, "Hmmm, we've not ever had that objection before."

We are indeed genuinely concerned and we try to meet their needs on any reasonable level. Of course, there are times when it's impossible to please some clients.

Drop everything and come out right now!

One client, although nice, literally stood over my shoulder the entire cleaning. While I was cleaning, she even "helped" me by pointing out all the spots I missed. She stood so close behind me that I elbowed her a couple times. I politely asked for some space so I could clean, but she didn't lighten up.

Several months later, she called on a Monday morning. Blue Windex concentrate had spilled on her carpet and she needed me NOW! I told her how we normally are booked up a week or two in advance, but we could squeeze her in later that afternoon.

Now it gets weird. She insisted I reschedule my appointments for later and come to her house right now. "Your other clients will understand," she said.

After explaining that it was not possible

to reschedule my entire day, I gave her some emergency spot removal tips, and assured her that coming this afternoon will have just as much likelihood of stain removal if she follows my advice. "If you can't be here within the next hour, I'll have to start using another cleaning company," was her reply.

With that, I let her know that she is important to us, but the best I could do was to come out later that same afternoon. I apologized that we couldn't help her and ended the conversation.

You can't make everyone happy. But, do everything you can to please your clients, let all of them know you appreciate them, and that you want to make them happy. Sometimes you're faced with the impossible.

Urine man

When a client is moving into a new house, and there's an odor, beware. This client spent nearly an hour talking to me on the phone about our urine removal process. I clearly told him we couldn't guarantee to remove all odors with the carpet cleaning process alone.

He needed cleaning done right away because he was moving in soon. When my technician did the estimate, he stated that additional odor removal may be needed after cleaning.

This house was in a nice, older part of town. The ironic part was that we couldn't find urine with our urine detector, but the client insisted it was urine. It only had a faint, older home smell. The client told my tech that another reputable company in town promised him 100% odor removal. To that, my tech smiled and said, "Then that's your man." He cordially left the premises.

The next morning, we got a call. It was urine

Pet accident.   Saturate with deodorization solution.   Extract with sub-surface extraction.   Clean carpet!

Urine removal can be very profitable once you know how to take care of the odor and communicate expectations with your client.

man. He said the other company came out, but they didn't seem professional, so he wanted to know if we could come out to do the job. As luck would have it, my same tech was cleaning in the neighborhood that afternoon. I reluctantly booked the job.

I personally went out to make sure all went well. The client was okay with signing our work order that stated, "NO GUARANTEES OR REFUNDS DUE TO ODOR. FURTHER ODOR TREATMENT MAY BE NEEDED AT ADDITIONAL COST."

Then, we cleaned and spent twice the time we normally would on a job this size. He watched over our shoulders. The client was happy. We got paid and left.

Two days later, we got a call. It was urine man. He said he still smelled an odor. I let him know of the other avenues to remove mystery odors and the costs associated with each. He was furious. He thought we should go out, clean it again, leave ozone machines, and spend another several hours at our expense.

I reminded him of the signed work order and that I already explained there would be additional costs. He said, "Yeah, you covered yourself really well, didn't you?" Then he hung up. I thought, yes I did. I'm glad I put that exclusion on the work order. Make sure you cover yourself with urine odor and other severe soiling problems.

Restaurant carpet nightmare

Toward the start of my business, the owner of a restaurant called. His carpet had not been cleaned in two years. I explained it would take a few cleanings to get it looking decent again, and that he had waited too long for cleaning. He understood and hired us.

We cleaned and cleaned. It looked better, but not good. After spending a couple of hours cleaning into the night, I called him and said we were done. We could have spent another eight hours and the carpet still wouldn't have looked great.

He looked around. I told him we weren't going to be able to finish and that he didn't owe me anything for tonight. He insisted to pay something, but I insisted that he didn't.

I learned a few things that night. One, I was making more per hour doing residential than restaurant carpet. Two, there are some jobs you shouldn't take at all or charge way more if it's really dirty. Three, restaurant carpet is nasty and not something I wanted to pursue.

Should you do commercial cleaning?

Sure, commercial can be great during slow months to keep your crews busy. Just make sure you go after the right commercial accounts. Restaurants typically aren't the best.

Target law firms, doctor offices, dentists, private schools, large office complexes, and other businesses that have money and need to keep their office looking great.

Property managers and apartment complexes can be good too, but you may have to weed through some bad ones. Charge what YOU need to charge and not what they want to pay. And don't put up with abuse.

> ## Carpet & Floor Cleaning So Perfect, It's a No Brainer!
>
> I'll Show You How to Get the CLEANEST OFFICE CARPET & FLOORS in Pensacola and Do it So Easily You'd Be Crazy Not To Call Me!
>
> Dear Client name,
>
> Why did I send you a small brain in this letter?
>
> First, to draw your attention to this short message.
>
> Second, I know what its like to have a 'sure-thing' staring you in the face; a "No-Brainer." I've been there. I've passed up on other opportunities or advice that I wish I had taken.
>
> I don't want you make the same mistakes I've made!
>
> I can help you in one of three ways:
>
> 1. You'll get our best special offers for cleaning since **you're a commercial facility in a neighborhood** we often service. Call now for a special offer you're going to LOVE.
>
> 2. **FAST service** since you're in an area we often service, we can often get to you FAST and EFFICIENTLY (also because you're our neighbor).
>
> 3. FREE follow up spot cleaning! Once you're our client, we want to offer you ONE **FREE spot removal** any time over the next year.
>
> If Any Of Those Above Reasons Sound Like a 'No-Brainer,' Continue Reading!

An attention-getting sales letter is one of the best ways to gain attention of the decision maker of a commercial account.

Here's an entire commercial marketing plan you can download. **www.hitmanadvertising.com/blog/commercial-marketing-plan**

What do you do when a client demands a discount?

The customer's always right. Or not? Actually, that idea of the customer being always right came from a marketing person who meant that the customer is always right in what they want, so you should sell them what they want.

It does NOT mean that you should lie down and give your customer whatever they want. If you did that, you'd surely go broke.

When a customer demands a discount, we want to know why they feel entitled to a discount. Normally the request for a discount comes when you've given them an estimate and before you start cleaning.

Keep in mind, the mere fact that they want a discount means they are sold on your company. Normally, a request for a discount is done only to check to see if you'll cave in on your price.

First, we'll stand our ground and tell them there are no discounts. If they have already responded to a special offer, we tell them that the special offer they already have is the best discount we have right now (assuming that really is the case). If they haven't been given a discount yet, we may tell them about our current special offer. This makes most people happy.

There are a few "bargain" clients who will continue to demand a discount. It's important to understand why. If you've told them your current special offer and they still want a discount further, you may want to outright ask how much they want to spend on cleaning.

If they want to pay $200 and you quoted them $300, strip down the service to $200. For example, if your $300 quote included the entire house of carpet cleaning with some furniture moving, figure what it would cost to clean the entire house minus two of the seldom-used bedrooms to see if that comes closer to $200.

Perhaps, omitting the furniture moving from the living room will bring the cost down. Do something to meet them at $200.

When you approach your client with removing some of your service, you prove to be more professional and your pricing structure is more real. In fact, we may even pull out our price list and give it to them. At this point, our job is to get the job down to only $200 based on our price list.

We need a reason to bring the price down.

Were we late? Did we have a spot that returned last time and the client never called for a follow up? Did we do anything wrong? If not, there's no reason to give an additional discount. Instead, we stick with stripping away and lessening the amount of service we're giving them.

If it comes down to this…my technicians are instructed to tell our clients that they aren't allowed to do any cleaning for less than the price sheet. In fact, my techs know they occasionally clean for one of my friends who may test them on this. The tech will tell the client that he could get in big trouble for reducing the price.

Even if you are the tech, who happens to be the owner, create a price sheet and go by your set prices.

Sample phone script for incoming calls

This is a script similar to what I used in my carpet cleaning business. Adapt one for your business so questions aren't forgotten and you don't get stumped by random question

"ABC Carpet Cleaning, this is _____, how can I help you?"

Gather initial information:
"Great, have you used us before?"

"Where did you hear about us?"

"Are we going to be cleaning just a few rooms or the whole house?"

"How many square feet is your entire home? Or, do you know the room dimensions?"

"Let me tell you a little bit about what we can do for you:"

"First, we've got a great REPUTATION in the area. Many realtors and flooring stores recommend us (name a few) because they know we go above and beyond your average cleaning company."

"Here's what we do in our SYSTEM:"

1. Your carpet is pre-vacuumed with a high powered commercial vacuum.

2. Edge vacuumed along baseboards to remove any dust and animal dander.

3. All the areas get pre-sprayed with an all natural cleaning agent to break down stuck in oils and dirt.

4. Then we'll use 12 specialty spotters for any problem stains...

5. More information gathering: What type of problems are you having with your carpet, tile, etc? Spots? Odors?

6. After your spots are treated, your carpet is cleaned with our truck mounted machine attached to our "Drimaster" system that rinses your carpet with 180 degree water and is designed to remove almost all of the water used so your carpet is left freshly rinsed and nearly dry. Fast drying with steam cleaning means spots aren't as likely to return and it's better for your carpet.

7. Last, we'll bring in a turbo air mover to speed dry one room that you want dry the fastest.

"No other company gives you the guarantees we do."

1. You'll get a 30 day no spots returning guarantee on carpet.

2. If any other company can remove a spot that we can't, we'll reimburse you for paying that company.

3. "If you're not happy, it's FREE" If you're not happy with what we've done after we clean a small test area, we'll leave and you owe us nothing! (Does not apply to spot removal jobs or to specialty problems)

Final information gathering:

"Will we be moving furniture for you, or cleaning around furniture? Are we cleaning any rooms upstairs?"

"Normally, we give you a rough estimate on the phone. Based on the information you gave me, you have about _____ square feet of carpet.

We'll give an exact quote before we begin, so this is a ballpark so you know an approximate cost."

"To clean _____ sq ft, the price would be _____."

"Did you want to book an appointment for as soon as possible, or do you have a certain day in mind?"

Run a real business

Create a price sheet. Write out a marketing plan. Write up a phone script. Put together a policies and procedures book for your employees or future employees if you don't currently have employees.

Most cleaning businesses fail to make the money they deserve due to lack of planning. Start planning now.

Chapter 6:

Conclusion

Plan your carpet cleaning business for massive success

If you fail to plan, you plan to fail. You don't begin a journey without a goal in mind. Otherwise, how will you know when you've gotten to where you want to go?

Most business owners make this mistake. Since the carpet cleaning business is very hands on type work, we get so busy we often forget to plan. Someone always needs a last minute cleaning because their dog vomited on their new carpet. Great. That's what you're in business for. But make sure you take the time to work on growing your business so your business will prosper.

Do you want to stay where you are? Or, do you want to grow? Or, do you want to be more involved in the office and less involved in actual cleaning?

Here are some questions to ask yourself and write down

(Yes, write it down now)

How much do I want to make in gross sales (total sales) next month?

How much do I want to profit next month?

How much do I want to make in gross sales (total sales) next year?

How many trucks do I need on the road?

How many employees do I need to get the cleaning jobs done?

What marketing tactics will I do to get this amount of sales done?

    Tracking your profit is crucial. It doesn't matter if you're doing $100k in sales every month if you're spending $110k to get the sales. Profit is all that matters in the business world. Track it. Set a monthly goal for profit.

    Here's a great way to increase gross sales. Pay your employees a bonus if your sales goals are met. Track your sales every day and post your numbers on a marker board. Some entrepreneurs are afraid to give their employees a sales total. But you know what? They're doing it anyway. They can tell how much you're making.

Most successful corporations do this. It inspires employees to have a goal for bigger sales. Plus, it makes them feel like they're a part of a group project.

If you run several crews, your crews will actually compete against each other to see who has the highest sales for the day. Every crew competes to be the highest producing for the day or week. All the while, you increase your gross sales. It works like magic.

If your employees want to make a set amount of money every week, design a commission or bonus based salary. The plan should be derived in a way that allows your employee to meet their goals and you to meet yours. It's a win-win proposal.

What should you plan?

Plan for the right amount of employees. At first, you may be the only employee. Too many employees can hurt your profit. As well, too few employees can hurt sales. Add employees when needed. Consider how many employees it will take to get your jobs done efficiently.

After you figure the ideal number of employees, make it a goal to keep your set amount for the next month.

Plan to win. Set daily, weekly, monthly, and yearly goals. Let your employees know some of them, but keep some to yourself.

Plan out your marketing. Take an hour to write out a complete marketing plan. This will give you more ideas and help you feel more secure about getting business. If you envision it, you can do it.

Create a plan to get a constant stream of referrals coming from current clients and businesses who can refer you. Referrals don't happen by accident.

You have to be different

Chances are, your city doesn't need another carpet cleaner. They need a carpet cleaner with a special niche, a special offer, or a unique selling proposition. Only companies who dare to be different make an impact on a market.

Think about your favorite restaurant. Do you go there because it's just like the others? Do you go there because it's the cheapest place in town? Probably not. There's something special there.

Sure there are consumers who are only interested in cheap cleaning services. That's fine. Don't bother convincing them otherwise. I suggest you move on to targeting homeowners and businesses who really care about a quality cleaning service and who will gladly give you tons of money.

Once you've come up with a way to differentiate yourself, market it. Consumers will gladly give you their hard earned money and thank you for your services.

It doesn't matter if you fail

Failure is not an option. Most millionaires have failed. You may fail. That's okay. I failed at my first attempt and I failed at several other things I attempted. But a successful person realizes that failure is an event. It's something that happened and then it's done. You can start over.

You are NOT a failure if you fail. You're just figuring out how to do it the right way. If running a successful cleaning business was easy, we'd have a lot more people getting into the cleaning business. There is a lot to test and learn.

Persistence is what matters

One of the biggest success traits I've learned is persistence. If at first you don't succeed, try again and again. No big deal. So, keep at it.

Don't quit! I believe in you. You can do it.

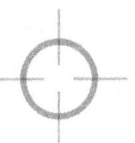

"Don't quit. Never give up trying to build the world you can see, even if others can't see it. Listen to your drum and your drum only. It's the one that makes the sweetest sound."-

Simon Sinek

Me With My First Cleaning Van

I just wanted to be an entrepreneur. I didn't want a real job. Starting a carpet cleaning company turned out to be harder than any job, but more profitable and with more freedom than I imagined.

Put in the work to grow your business and you'll reap the rewards.

A Few More Marketing Examples

Emergency Spot Removal

1. **DO IT NOW** to prevent permanent stains
2. **Remove solid** substances with a spoon
3. **Extract liquid** with a wet vacuum machine
4. **Treat with a mild** carpet spotter
5. **Rinse spotter** out with water

If stain persists, call **XXX-XXXX** or visit Yourwebsite.com

PREMIUM Carpet Care

If you're going to create a magnet, you may as well give your clients something that can help them...and something they're not as likely to throw away. Clients love these and they'll stick them on a fridge, washing machine, or cabinet just to save your spotting tips.

Educate your clients about WHY they're having the problems they are having. Of course, you are the solution to their problems. This type of educational marketing is NEVER wasted money. It builds your reputation as a professional and builds up your brand. Do this and your clients won't forget you.

Send your clients a thank you note after their cleaning. The photo above is a thank you postcard to send clients. It's a 4x6 inch postcard, so it's sent with the cheaper postcard stamp. It's quick and cost effective and it goes WAY above what the average carpet cleaner does for their clients.

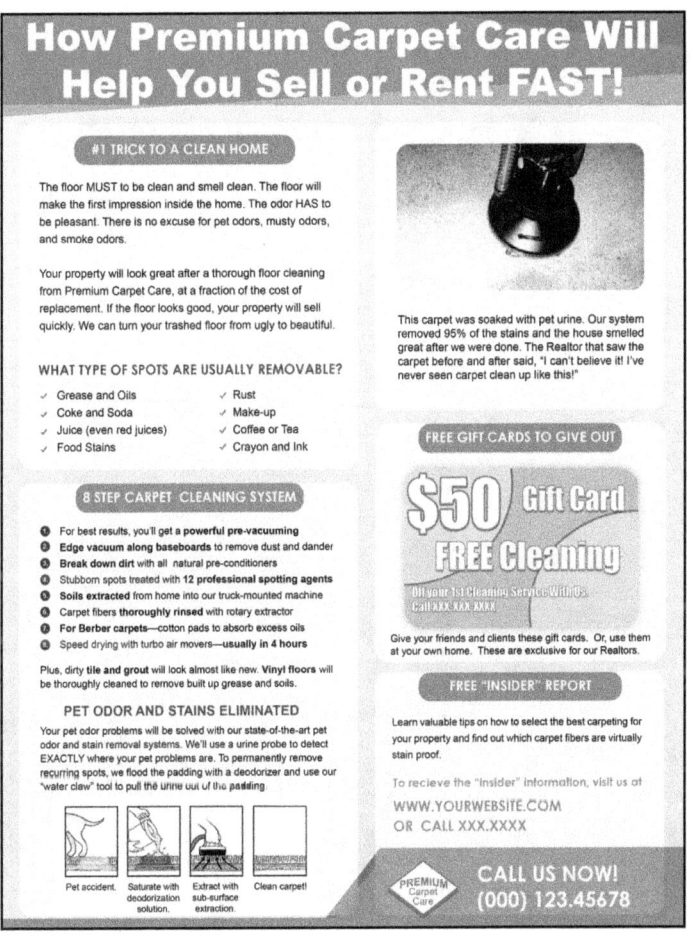

When you're marketing to realtors and property managers, give them benefits and offers specific to them. You want them on your side.

FREE Marketing Plan

Get my FREE, updated marketing plan. The media and tips I recommend change frequently. If you'd like an updated plan with ad examples in full color, sign up for my email newsletter at **www.Hitmanadvertising.com**

If you've already signed up for my email newsletter, just put your email address and name in again and you'll be forwarded to the page with the marketing plan download.

If you need immediate help with your advertising, call us at **850-474-1110** or send us a message over on our dedicated support page at **www.Hitmanadvertising.com/support**

Facebook Group

Join in on the conversation about cleaning marketing on Facebook. It's FREE. Request to join here.

www.facebook.com/groups/cleaningmarketing

For a List of Resources Recommended in this book, go to.

www.Hitmanadvertising.com/resources

What's Your Plan for Success in the Cleaning Business?

Other Books by John Braun

These books are available on Amazon or by visiting **www.Hitmanadvertising.com**

Killer Advertising for Cleaning Businesses. Published 2016.

Secrets of Highly Profitable Advertising. Published 2017.

Cleaning Marketing E-Newsletter. Sign up FREE at **www.Hitmanadvertising.com**

HitMan Advertising

Target Clients Profitably

Contact John at **850-474-1110**

Or **www.Hitmanadvertising.com/support**

www.ingramcontent.com/pod-product-compliance
Lightning Source LLC
Chambersburg PA
CBHW070646220526
45466CB00001B/313